If Animals Built Your House

Words by Bill Wise

Pictures by Rebecca Evans

To my sons, Bill and Cam. Love, Dad.

—BW

For Eden, Reese, and Jensen from the best Aunt Bee ever!

—RE

Text © 2021 by Bill Wise

Illustrations © 2021 by Rebecca Evans

Cover and internal design © 2021 by Sourcebooks

Cover design by Jackie Cummings/Sourcebooks

Internal Images © Backiris/Getty Images, Simon Greig/Shutterstock, Marina Vedernikova/Getty Images, Nick Pitsas/Creative Commons 3.0, Anup Shah/Getty Images, Kapenta/Creative Commons 4.0, Joseph C Boone/Creative Commons 4.0, Johnny Johnson/Getty Images, Santiago Urquijo/Getty Images

Published by Dawn Publications, an imprint of Sourcebooks eXplore

P.O. Box 4410, Naperville, Illinois 60567-4410

(630) 961-3900

sourcebookskids.com

Library of Congress Cataloging-in-Publication Data is on file with the publisher.

Source of Production: Wing King Tong Paper Products Co. Ltd., Shenzhen, Guangdong Province, China

Date of Production: November 2021

Run Number: 5024171

Printed and bound in China.

WKT 10 9 8 7 6 5 4 3

If animals built your house, would you want to live in it?

If a tree squirrel built your house,
no one could ever sneak up on you.

Your house might look like just a jumble of leaves, but it's really a tightly woven, waterproof ball. No hard walls here—this furry builder used its body like a rolling pin to make a soft, cozy room. Just watch out for that first step out your front door!

If **mound termites** built your house, you'd always have friends to hang out with—two million of them!

You'd live in the tallest structure built by animals—created by tiny architects no bigger than a grain of rice. Your tower would be made of dried mud, saliva, and poop sturdy enough to last for one hundred years. Don't get lost in the dark tunnels!

If a red grouper built your house, you'd never have to take off your scuba gear.

This hard worker excavated sand to get down to hard rock on the ocean floor. But the grouper didn't need a digger and dump truck to do the job—it used its mouth! It not only built a house for you, but for your neighbors too. How do you feel about sharing your room with a lobster?

If a colony of honeybees built your house, you could scoop gobs of honey off your walls.

You'd have to squeeze into a super tiny room, tightly packed next to thousands of others. It could get deadly hot inside, but don't worry. Worker bees would spend hours fanning their wings at 230 beats per second to cool it down.

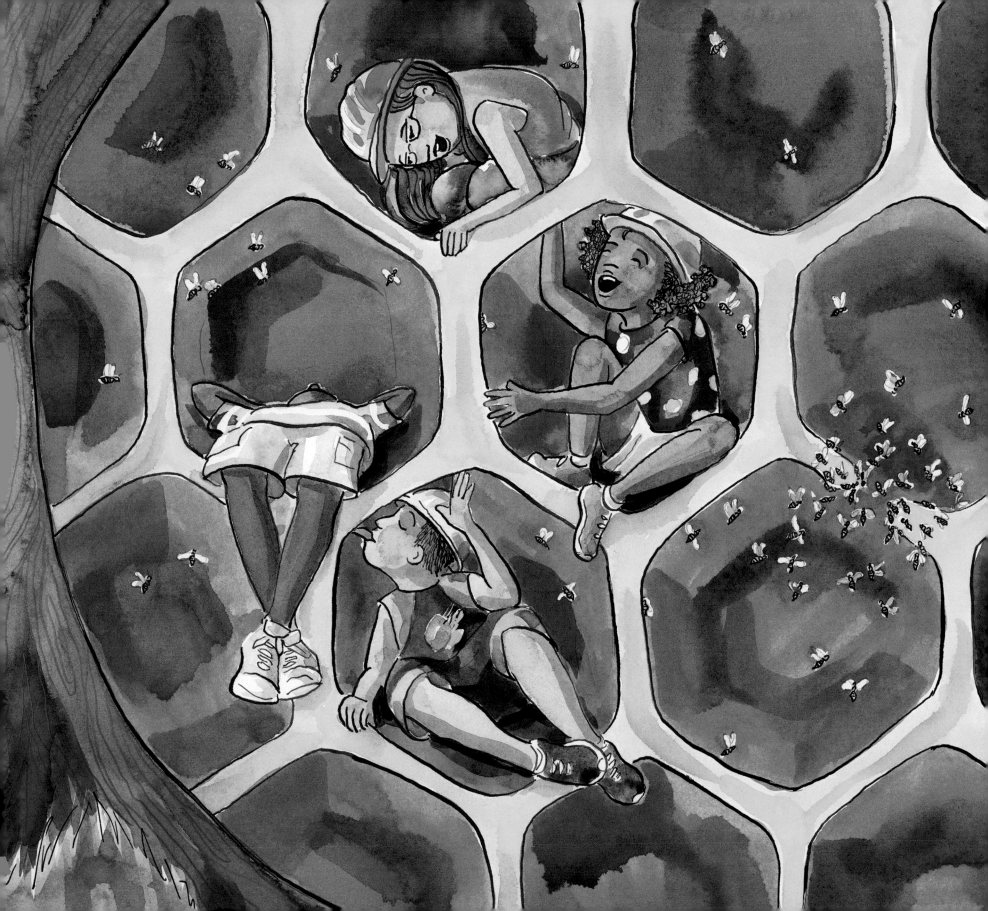

If a chimpanzee built your house, you'd snooze high in the rain forest canopy as leopards prowled below.

Chimps get lots of practice weaving comfy nests—they build a new one every night. That's 365 new nests every year! Once tucked into a cup of branches and leaves, you'd never have to worry about falling out. But you'd better bring an umbrella—your house doesn't have a roof.

If a foam-nest tree frog built your house, you'd be able to fish from your front door.

Your female builder would have produced a sticky liquid from her body and whipped it into foam with her legs to create your bubbly home. No jumping up and down in this house! In seven days, the floor will disintegrate and you'll fall into the pond below. Can you swim?

If a satin bowerbird built your house, you'd have the fanciest place on the block.

This bird is the ultimate artist of the animal kingdom. Hope you like blue—it's the satin bower bird's favorite color. You'd have blue stones, seeds, bottle caps, and even blue straws decorating your yard. Twig walls would be coated with special paint—chewed up berries mixed with bird saliva.

If a polar bear built your house, you'd live under a dazzling display of northern lights.

Using her huge paws, your Arctic architect would have carved you a snug cave in the deep snow. Hope you like to take long naps because once you crawl in, you'll be there for the entire winter. Better bring your mittens so you can dig your way out in the spring!

If alligators built your house, you'd have two styles to choose from.

Is relaxing in a hot sauna your idea of fun? Then you might want a female alligator to build your house—a nest of rotting plants is always hot and wet. Or maybe you prefer to submerge yourself in a gator hole—an underwater tunnel made by a male alligator. Take your pick!

If a pack rat built your house, you'd never have to clean your room.

Pack rat houses are always a mess! You'd live in a tangle of sticks, rocks, and plants cemented together with pack-rat pee. You'd never know what your living room would look like because these hoarders would add something new each night—everything from junk to jewelry. Shiny is best!

If beavers built your house, you'd be living inside an island in the middle of a pond.

Beavers are more than just builders—they're environmental engineers. Before they built your stick home, they first had to make a pond. Now that's what you call waterfront property! Don't forget where to find the secret underwater entrance.

So, what kind of house would YOU build?

Critter Construction
What and Why Animals Build

Tree squirrels build a *drey*—a tightly woven nest of twigs, leaves, and moss. A soft lining of shredded bark keeps babies safe and warm.

Wild **honeybees** often build a *hive* inside a hollow tree. Worker bees shape wax into six-sided cells to form a honeycomb. The cells are used to store honey and pollen and raise larvae.

Mound termites build a *mound* that's taller than a giraffe! The termite colony lives underground in a huge network of tunnels. The mound circulates fresh air and protects the colony.

Chimpanzees build sleeping *nests* to keep warm at night and stay safe from predators. They make a platform of branches and cover it with leaves, using the softest ones for a pillow.

Red groupers dig cave-like *holes* in the sea floor to attract mates and lure prey. Their house sites create habitats for sponges, corals, shrimp, lobsters, and other sea creatures.

Grey foam-nest tree frogs lay thousands of eggs in a bubbly *nest*. After the eggs hatch, the nest breaks apart. The tadpoles drop into the water below and continue to develop into frogs.

A male **satin bowerbird** creates a *bower*—two walls made out of sticks with a lane in between. Using the inside of the bower like a stage, he performs a song and dance to attract females.

Pack rats that live in the desert make a *den* in and around cactus plants, which shelters them from extreme heat and provides a safe place to raise their young. Cactus spines deter predators.

Polar bears live in one of the harshest places on the planet—the Arctic. A female digs out a *cave* in a snowbank to create a den—a safe place to give birth and raise her cubs.

Beaver *lodges* keep babies and the whole family safe from predators. Beavers are some of the world's best ecosystem engineers because their dams dramatically change the environment.

A female **alligator** lays her eggs in a *nest* to keep them safe and warm. Eggs from warmer nests hatch as females, and eggs from cooler nests hatch as males.

Animals build for survival. They need safe places to give birth and raise their young. Their structures give them shelter from harsh weather and protection from predators. Some houses help them attract a mate or catch food.

Literacy Connection

Read-Aloud Suggestions

1. Begin by reading the title and the name of the author and illustrator. Ask: What kinds of houses do animals build? List responses on the board.

2. Read the book all the way through without stopping, except to clarify word meanings if necessary.

3. When finished, compare the houses in the book with the students' list, adding any new types of houses.

4. Read aloud and discuss the information in "Explore More for Kids." Have students share their own personal experiences with animals and houses mentioned in the book or with any they've seen locally, such as bird nests or ant hills.

5. The last page of the story asks the question: What kind of house would YOU build? The STEAM Challenge gives students an opportunity to answer this question by designing a house with the help of an animal.

Fact or Fiction—Take a Closer Look

Animals building houses for people is a fantastical idea—it's fiction. But the information about the houses is true—it's factual. Combining both fact and fiction raised a lot of questions for the illustrations: What size will the animals be in relation to the kids? Will the houses be shown their actual size or kid-sized? How will the kids be shown inside the houses? Should the houses be shown in their actual habitats and locations around the world? How will the kids get from house to house?

There isn't "one right way" to answer these questions. It's up to the illustrator to decide how to make fact and fiction work together in a fun and creative way. Have students look carefully at the illustrations to determine how illustrator Rebecca Evans answered the questions. You may have them work in small groups and then discuss their ideas with the whole class.

Illustration Answers—The relative sizes of the animals compared to the kids are accurate (fact). No matter how big or small the animal is shown, they built a "kid-sized" house (fiction). Many of the houses are shown with a cut-away view with the kids inside. The interiors of these houses are accurate (fact), but most of them are enlarged so the kids can fit inside (fiction). All of the animals are building the houses in a brand-new subdivision (fiction). Each house is shown in the habitat where it actually exists in the wild (fact). Locating all of the habitats in one subdivision allows the kids to move quickly and easily from house to house.

More Illustration Fun

🏠 Notice the mailbox for each house. How does it relate to the animal that built the house?

🏠 What is the name of the subdivision? Brainstorm other names that would fit the story.

🏠 In each illustration, find the house from the previous page and the hint for the house that will be featured on the next page.

🏠 Using the map, trace the route the kids followed. What are all of the different habitats shown within the subdivision?

Science Connection

Building for Survival

Animals are amazing architects and engineers! Using only their bodies and the natural materials found in their environment, they build houses that help them survive. The basic survival needs of all animals are air, food, water, space (habitat), and shelter. Some animals, such as termites and honeybees, work together for the survival of a large group rather than just for their individual survival.

The information in "Critter Construction" briefly explains how these survival needs are met. Interested students can discover more fascinating facts about the animals and their houses online.

Some animal homes have very little impact on the environment, while others completely alter it. For example, a chimpanzee nest is used for just one night, but a beaver lodge is used for generations. Animals that significantly impact the environment and strongly affect other animals and plants are called ecosystem engineers. They're also known as a keystone species because the habitat would drastically change if that species were removed. The keystone species in this book are the alligator, beaver, grouper, and honeybee.

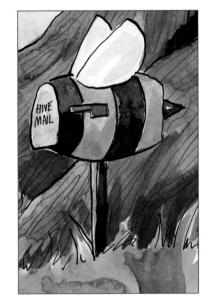

STEAM Challenge

For this STEAM challenge, students will design a house that answers the question on the last page of the story: What kind of house would YOU build? Below is a summary of the components of the challenge.

Study Nature—Students will research animal homes by observing local animals, reading books, and watching online videos. Have students notice the natural materials each animal uses for its home.

Design a Home—The last page of the story shows children building a house with the help of an animal. For example, the beaver is helping a boy build his mud hut because a beaver lodge is made with mud. Bowerbirds are helping a girl decorate her teepee with blue stones and paint, just as they do with their bower. Have students brainstorm possible designs for their own house and an animal that could help them build it.

Create a Model—Engineers build models, and so do many artists! Have students decide on a house design and provide them with a variety of natural materials and craft supplies to make a model of it. Alternately, students may draw a picture of their house and animal helper.

Present to Others—Host an "Open House" for students to share their pictures or models. They can describe the special features of their house explaining the reasons why they would like to live in it and how the animal would have helped them build it.

Make a Mailbox—A fun illustration feature in the book is a mailbox related to the animal and/or its environment. Invite students to include a personalized mailbox that especially fits their house design. Alternately, creating a mailbox with natural and recycled materials can be used as a stand-alone activity.

Bill Wise has a passion for sports, nature, and mathematics. Inspired to combine these interests, he wrote his first book for Dawn, *If You Played Hide-and-Seek with a Chameleon*. The same group of five adventurous kids are also featured in this book as they discover the amazing engineering and architectural skills of twelve different animals. Bill lives in Maine with his wife, Mary Ann. Now that he's retired from teaching middle school, Bill enjoys writing full time. Visit him at bwiseauthor.com.

Rebecca Evans started drawing as soon as she could hold a crayon and just never stopped. After working for nine years as an artist and designer, she returned to her first love—children's book illustration. She's authored and/or illustrated twenty books; this is her fourth book for Dawn. Rebecca is also a Regional Co-Advisor for her SCBWI chapter. She lives in Maryland and enjoys spending time with her husband and four young children, while working from her home studio during every spare moment. Find her at rebeccaevans.net.

Also by Bill Wise and Illustrated by Rebecca Evans

If You Played Hide-and-Seek with a Chameleon—What would happen if you played games with animals? Sports, science, and math come together in twelve outrageous competitions. Win or lose, it's hilarious fun!

More Dawn Books Illustrated by Rebecca Evans

Why Should I Walk? I Can Fly!—A little bird, a big sky, and the first time out of the nest! A robin's first flight is a gentle reminder about what we can accomplish if we just keep trying.

Plants Fight Back—Plants are part of every food chain, which means lots of animals want to eat them. But plants "fight back" with clever adaptations that help them survive.

May We Also Recommend These Nature Awareness Books

Scampers Thinks Like a Scientist—Scampers is no ordinary mouse—she knows how to investigate. Her infectiously experimental spirit will have young readers eager to think like scientists too!

There's a Bug on My Book—All sorts of critters hop, fly, wiggle, and slide across the pages of this book, engaging children's imaginations while introducing them to the animals in the grass beneath their feet.

Pass the Energy, Please!—Everyone is somebody's lunch. In this upbeat rhyming story, the food chain connects herbivores, carnivores, insects, and plants together in a fascinating circle of players.

Wonderful Nature, Wonderful You—Nature can be a great teacher. With a light touch especially suited to children, this twentieth anniversary edition evokes feelings of calm acceptance, joy, and wonder. A delight for all ages.

Dawn Publications is dedicated to inspiring in children a deeper understanding and appreciation for all life on Earth.